A Dan Campion poem can step
    into the room
like that most insouciant of facts: Bogie

    came from
a blue chip family.
—Paul Carroll (1981, in "Walking to a Poetry Reading
by My Students")

Dan Campion's poetry reveals a formal sensibility that is unusual in poets today, particularly among the younger ones. The clear intelligence underlying them is apparent, and the sense of precision the work demonstrates—word by word and line by line—is impressive.
—Barry Silesky (1983, in a review of *Calypso*
in *Another Chicago Magazine*)

Campion's poetic evolution over the past twenty years is illuminating. Rooted in a rich tradition of Franco-Hispanic surrealism (he has contributed to a contemporary French-American anthology as well as *Hispanic Journal*), his early work shows an influence of what might be called "surrealist-collage," the clear statement of unrelated details and their juxtaposition, with the implication that the reader is to assemble them.

This influence, which goes back at least as far as Baudelaire, Nerval, and Rimbaud, Campion has never entirely abandoned, which is all to the good. They give his formal advances, in the late eighties and nineties, a ragged energy and dense detailing unique in contemporary poetry....

Campion's poems, like all such deeply innovative work, are deeply traditional, *radical* in their reaching back, down, beneath the real, to language's slippery roots, sly morphemes. "This way," say the signposts, "to magic, this way madness. This way, sanity."

Witty, slangy, elliptical, funny, Campion's poems are above all *readable*. They're work; but they're nice work (if you can get it). They're difficult in the way that poems should be difficult: Not arbitrarily, not from the laziness or caprice of indolent authordom, but because of the inherent nature of their subject matter....

 Campion's poems have surfaced in a multitude of periodicals (everything from *Oink!* to *Rolling Stone* to *Poetry*; though there's only one collection of his verse). He's one of a number of relatively young poets who are formidable technicians, and have constructed thereby that quality impossible to fake, an individual voice. His poems are dense relicts of deep interior acts, iron-shavings combed out into graceful patterns by the magnetism at the core.

—John Mella (1998, in Light)

In *The Mirror Test*, Dan Campion's poems inspire time & reflection, asking to be read & contemplated slowly, quietly. Their beauty, simplicity/complexity astound.

 These are words of substance—perceptive, transient, brilliantly composed—where nature, geography, & art give us solace & insight, & the mirrors pose questions asking us to look inside/outside ourselves.

 These are words of "The Deep Field," a "blaze orange T-shirt," & "the suit of lights" where "A moment's stillness is allowed."

 From sparrow to narwhal to dragonfly to bear to Stellar's jay, with his keen eye & detailed, rich imagery & allusions, Campion requires us to enter language. His poems like rafts—allow us glimpses into & beyond the natural world, connecting us to love, loss, & survival—as we journey through water & land & sky—voyagers all.

—Marcia Arrieta

The Mirror Test

The Mirror Test

Dan Campion

MadHat Press
Cheshire, Massachusetts

MadHat Press
MadHat Incorporated
PO Box 422, Cheshire, MA 01225

Copyright © 2024 Dan Campion
All rights reserved

The Library of Congress has assigned
this edition a Control Number of
2024936972

ISBN 978-1-952335-79-2 (paperback)

Words by Dan Campion
Cover image: *Décollage* by Marc Vincenz, Jake Quatt
& Sophia Santos
Cover design by Marc Vincenz

www.MadHat-Press.com

First Printing
Printed in the United States of America

For JoAnn

The mirror test was developed by psychologist Gordon Gallup Jr. in 1970 as a method for determining whether a non-human animal has the ability of self-recognition.

—Animalcognition.org

[P]oetry is an everlasting Ark, / ... bearing and begetting all the mind's animals.

—Delmore Schwartz, "The Kingdom of Poetry"

The world should not be understood as an amorphous ensemble of atoms—but rather as a game of mirrors, founded on the correlations between the structures formed by combinations of these atoms.

—Carlo Rovelli, *Reality Is Not What It Seems,* translated by Simon Carnell and Erica Segre

Table of Contents

I. Gichigami

Gichigami	3
Hands	5
Softness Itself	6
The Purple Finch	7
Rosehill Park	8
Beginning Again	9
The Narwhal	10
Deep Field	11
Breton Sound	12
Peregrine, Crocus, Aquavit	13
Fireflies	14
Picacho Peak	15
Grief	16
Quick Studies	17
Exposure	18
Pied-à-terre	19
Suffusion	20
Correction	21
Redwing	22
The Salamander	23
Jubilate Lupo	24
Turtles	26
Coming Out of Hibernation	27
The Fascination of Fish	28
The Fountain of Beira	29
The Hall	30

II. Blaze Orange

Blaze Orange	33
Sleeping Dogs	34
Salt	35

Noël	36
Canvas	37
Salvation	38
The Hunting in Hunting	39
The Gathering	40
Traje de Luces	41
Late	42
The Raft of the Géricaults	43
Necessity	44
The Sleeping Gypsy	45
Canadas	46
The Ant	47
To Dwell by Water	48
The Two Dogs	49
Six Robins	50
Ice Fishing	51
The Shadows of the Raptors	52
Sharpshin	53
The Entry of the Dogs into Valhalla	54
The Hunt	55
Who'll Be Chief Scorner?	57
Three Elegies	59
Composition	60
Old Men Fishing	61

III. The Mirror Test

The Mirror Test	65
Crows	66
Tables	67
Interference	68
"Semantic and Poetic Meaning"	69
The Krater	70
Dalí's Daughter	71
Sonic Smith	72
Yanhuitlán	73
Ode in a Grecian Urn	74

Train of Thought	76
Opposing Thumb	78
Admiration	79
Erik Satie at the Debut of Claude Debussy's *La Mer*	80
The Cardinal	81
Joint Account	82
Automatic Writing	83
The Pomegranate	84
The Dragonfly	85
Schrödinger's Dog	86
The Cedar Berries	87
Poem for Daylight	88
Incantation	89
Glass Fish	90
Mr. Lucky	91
Dreams Are of the Body	92

IV. The Art of Representation

The Art of Representation	95
Hokusai in Iowa	96
The Fishers	98
The Exile of Glass	99
Muse	100
Point and Shoot	101
Admonitions	102
All Your Time	103
Deflection's Ode	105
A Book Dealer's Triptych	107
The Subject	108
Former Tenants	109
Archetype	110
A Kylix for the Boston Museum	111
Our Picture with Picasso	112
On Aging	113
The Fruiterer	114
Needles	115

Ovid's Metamorphosis	116
Capture	117
Fedora	118
The Picabia Skirt	119
Assistant	120
Street Views	121
Still	122
Scroll	123
Acknowledgments	125
About the Author	127

I. Gichigami

I think I could turn and live with animals,
they are so placid and self-contain'd, ...

—Walt Whitman, "Song of Myself"

Gichigami

Shark-visaged—don't trust me, go check the map—
Superior could scarf down Paumanok,
could swallow-whole Key Largo and Key West.
That's just in outline. Fleshed-out version means
you don your mask and dive where Longfellow
had no license to go: the freighters drowned,
the icecap's gouge, the sludge of modern use.
And while you're down there, wave and wind and sun
remake the picture-perfect topside lake
that painters paint and minnows navigate,
which, expert now, you can't appreciate;
it's just a landscape, water, skinny shore,
a play of light on surface, nothing more,
like Mississippi River to Mark Twain
when pilot training de-romanced that stream.
Except, of course, he had the memory still
of fresh eyes' first impression, of that thrill
Lucretius says we'll feel, observing stars,
by feigning we have not seen sky before.
It helps to tell a story: A great lake
much larger than Superior once rolled
to north and west. Glacial Lake Agassiz,
the dons called it, naming it for a don.
Superior and Agassiz, comrades
unvexed by humans, giants in deep time—
but you know this story, how one friend wastes,
dies, passes into other forms, is mourned
until new interests measure out relief.
No need to call in willing disbelief

Dan Campion

when lake with lost companion, famished, scarred,
is of our kind, shark, mimic, mourner, bard.

Hands

Your knuckles are curled
over the chair's arm
like a row of small observatories,
Palomar, Kitt Peak, Wilson, Yerkes,
seen from high altitude.
Cup your hand and whisper
toward it: the dish at Arecibo.
You're telling it nothing
new. And it's child's play
to pick one hand up
with the other as though
it were no part of you,
but rather the breast
of a small, upward-looking bird,
and, thinking of the fork
that holds it while
the knife goes singing through,
to pick out the violets
that cast their shadows on the bone.
The hand, both architect
and architecture, familiar
and furiously distant,
is still within the grasp
of your terrible face,
whose eyelids are beating like wings.

Softness Itself

That sandpiper doing the cakewalk
once was a man whose stripes
ran off his pants like water.
One striking thing about waterbirds,
or any birds for that matter, or
any water, is softness itself. Take for example
six different kinds of birds, or waters,
like beltloops around a woman's waist;
arrange them in a circle, which your eyes
divide one loop to a segment like a piece of pie.
Plug in to a passing siren
and watch the segments spin kaleidoscopically
to the rhythm of the street;
languid, nervous, violent or ridiculous
depending on where your feet happen to be.
A bird will fly by during all this activity
whose man once swam to safety,
a dove softly clutched in his teeth.

The Purple Finch

We identified the bird Palm Sunday
By a little leafing through the field guide.
("Like a sparrow dipped in raspberry juice"
Peterson aptly quotes some birder or,
For all we know, *Larousse Gastronomique*.)
The dried-blood sheen belongs to the male finch,
Which we watched pecking seed like a connoisseur
Among slovenly, morose house sparrows.
His appearance, sleek, intent, fastidious,
Was sharp and troubling in its novelty,
A new dimension nature meted out
For revelation like a René Magritte
Between the color of dried betel nuts
And the gore of a Flemish crucifixion.
We will surely dream of pomegranates,
Vin rouge, dark grapes, pink sacrificial flesh,
All the biblical and classical reds,
Before the rose-feathered memory fades.
The purple finch in regal plumage reigned,
And went away, and then a goldfinch came.

Rosehill Park

Two locusts sharp-thorned as briar,
Leafless as crows' feet,
Needle the heartshaped air.

Twists of leather in a brittle screed
Around them, acrid with tannin,
Filled with seed,

Crosshatch the dry grass,
Making endpapers of an heirloom book
Flowers filled last.

Across a pond ready to freeze,
Green walnuts blacken on the ground,
Their scent sharp as coffee.

The wasps' great paper heart,
Filled with falling shadows,
Lies, tilted, toward the coming dark.

Beginning Again

A starling clutching a locust branch
preens green wings in a green wind.
The lilacs bend,
an avalanche of heart-shaped leaves
in waning light and rain.
You must begin again.

The drumming on the roof
needs a name, a proof,
a sign someone could read.
Writing blank sheets,
rainwater cascades down the peak,
spills freely from the eaves.

High clouds redden.
The rain slacks off. The light dies.
A frost of stars spreads out
on a ragged field of sky.
The situation hasn't changed.
The scent of lilacs has arrived.

The Narwhal

Behind the glass it seemed to swim
aslant from us below the ice.
In light that seemed to penetrate
thick frost and freezing polar sea
the animation of its pose
asserted life against the dim-
lit mummies and sarcophagi,
museum trophies dug from sand
and placed beside our oceans' hall,
past which our crawling line had wound.
The ivory spindle of its horn
looked incorruptible, a lance
no shield could shatter or deflect.
No part of this great creature's girth
could be inurned or carapaced,
all purpose, freedom, movement, strength.
Its name, we must have thought, meant dread-
nought of the north, or northern whale.
Not so. The beast's named for its flesh,
which wears in life the dappled look
of drowned men's flesh, that floury gray,
hence, from *nár*, Norse corpse, "corpse whale."
A bookish hour, a hero flown:
the tusk is hollow, its use unknown.

Deep Field

The barest patch of loamy nighttime sky
is thickly sown with seedlike galaxies
the light from which no human eye can gather.
Across some distant field a nighthawk wavers.
His wing bars herringbone the bright moths' trails
as, photons in his wake, he seeks his prey.
Seated at this desk in my dark study
insulated from all expert gaze,
hidden from the hunters and their quarry,
I strew a page, and watch as red-shifts claim
first brave intention, then groundless fear,
until no paper's left; the blotter's clear.
Hard science plies that nebula, the mind,
as if it mattered. As, of course, it does,
our telescope above the atmosphere,
some say, or merest shadow of a hand
passing swiftly through a candle flame,
the vestige of cold stars that bore our name.

Breton Sound

Our continent dissolves here in mica.
The line through New Orleans and Baton Rouge
Connecting the Keys to the Placervilles
Can't arrow through this silt, but loops and coils,
Jazz improvisations on the river's
Phantom Illinois, whose Prophetstown's
At Little Rock. Just now, the flags relaxed,
The big veranda opened to the sun.
Black Bay flashes. The clouds and shores conspire,
All conversation swallowed up in light.

Five delicate fingers of nautical brass,
Palm unreadable in the tropical glare,
Some fragment of a vessel floats on sand.
Out of reach over the familiar cusp
Rises a second horizon, the world
Of conjury, a crescent city
Whitened by the sails of coca schooners.
A crane soars from one world toward the other,
While sandpipers, drawn with a soft blue point,
Evade the question, sibilants gliding.

Peregrine, Crocus, Aquavit

Shrunken head key chains,
magnetic mummies
in tinny cases,
plastic Tyrannosaurs:
the Olduvai Gorge,
Gobi Desert, and
Valley of the Kings
offered less than class
trips to the Field Museum
in the Eisenhower era.
Blue Bird school bus
caravans came home as
heavy with souvenirs
as Lord Carnarvon.
The boys chose crossbones,
kitsch like miniature skulls
smoking tiny cigarettes; the
girls took away clay beads,
quill pens, bright kerchiefs,
gems of quartz and glass,
and clutched stone phials
that might clasp
the waters of this life,
or any other.

Fireflies

They're few this year, like several seasons past.
You worry: Is it climate change? Disease?
Insecticides? And will the low count last,
or is it just there are dark years like these?
Remember when we lived on Prentiss Street,
a warm June dusk like this, I'd call you to
the window, where we'd watch a Xerxes' fleet
of lightboats swing their torches through the blue.
That house was disassembled long ago,
the crescent hill that cupped those bright arrays
built on, so where it was, you'd hardly know.
I'd drop a fortune to retrace the maze.
It doesn't stand still though. We can't go back.
And now, the blue hour gone, the air's just black.

Picacho Peak

A burro woke us from our fitful sleep
by shuffling around our tent at six
a.m., the temperature already steep,
our postures cramped as archaeopteryx
in stone from unaccustomed heat and air
too thin. We were not up for breakfast chores,
and you fell back asleep. On my own dare,
I rose, and started climbing on all fours
the switchbacks, almost vertical, that rose
above our campsite, up Picacho Peak.
Way up there, on a rocky ledge, I froze
as centipede long as my arm swept, beak
and claw, the scarp on which I'd leaned my head.
You'd fear I'd lost it, so I never said.

Grief

A single dove sits on the straight high wire,
her silhouette a soul by William Blake,
an Arnold Böcklin drape to her attire,
with seeming permanence no rough winds shake.
The sky is satin of Venetian make,
in silver with soft blue worked in the weave.
The dove wears deeper hue for mourning's sake
revealing no desire to ever leave.
But silk, wire, flesh, and hidden sun all grieve
for Grief herself, who nurses in her lair
the hurt she knows no unction can relieve
nor immemorial circumstances spare
and knows as sun proceeds and dove ascends
will outlive all the pleas her lover sends.

Quick Studies

The yearlings that cannot have seen it snow
before don't look surprised. Unlike a child,
they do not blink and ask, but simply know
this, too, befalls. They will not be beguiled.
It works for them, this instinct for the cold
acceptance of a falling, freezing sky.
It's possible that shelter's oversold
and wonder is a comically flat lie.
The woodlot isn't much to look at, sad
to say, thinned down by saw and ax and wedge.
Nobody stops here honing thoughts they've had.
In June, though, nestlings still are sure to fledge.
Quick studies at the craft of grays and blacks,
the ground fills up with snow, the snow with tracks.

Exposure

Each winter there's one sparrow on the ledge,
alone, that shivers more than all the rest
perched bobbing on their colony of sedge.
That it won't last a day seems manifest,
but morning dawns and he or she is back
again, plumped up against the cold and wet,
and pecking at the millet and the black
sunflower seed strewn on the parapet.
We might consider this lone sparrow death,
or fear of death, or wish for death, exposed,
indeed, half-frozen last breath,
but claws and beak still grip. It's death deposed.
And then comes spring and all the flock seems new
and never lets on which ones made it through.

Pied-à-terre

> *The birds begin to stir and wake, stillness becoming grace.*
> —JoAnn Castagna

Les moineaux—the sparrows—take to the air
so seeming effortlessly, like a breath
let out. Left back, I'm tending to their care:
seeds, shelter, bird bath to the proper depth.
They come back, stay awhile, decamp again
to who knows where. Their eyes do not recall,
and mine, too weak to trace out where they've been,
lock in denial they depart at all.
We craved, sometimes, a studio in town,
but never seemed quite far enough away.
Become your pied-à-terre, I'll get it down,
this harboring you any night or day,
without reservations, without stress,
whenever you're fatigued with wilderness.

Suffusion

Now that you are everywhere, you know
of course they've repaired Glendale Road, shored up
some trails in Hickory Hill, and tried to slow
erosion with wild grape and Indian cup.
Reciting what I've seen is so ingrained.
This morning when that doe and her two fawns
loped by I almost called you, but refrained.
It costs a beat when recollection dawns.
I watched them from the window where you stood
and saw the Cooper's hawk pluck flicker free
and carry her away toward deeper wood.
I hugged you as you wept. Now you hug me.
A goldfinch and a purple finch alight,
accept our offering, resume their flight.

Correction

After the first death, there is no other.
　　—Dylan Thomas

If he had outlived Caitlin by a year
he would have learned his error. Stars align,
sun slants, slate-colored juncos reappear,
and second death uncoils his dragon spine.
We are one flesh. I feel you recognize
the danger, tense your jaw, see no escape,
concede again the life they so much prize,
these Dracos, that they'll put on any shape.
When all their stratagems prevail, they'll starve,
the nest of them—whatever name we give
to snakes in plenty—no one there to carve
a scroll in stone to offspring still to live.
New death is what death-dates discover.
After the last death, there is no other.

Redwing

I knew your grandfather, I said. The red-
winged blackbird creaked back at me that no-song
that passes for an answer. Then he fled
up to a locust branch. *You don't belong,*
he said. *And leave my family out of this.*
I look only ahead. What could I do
but go my way. But I could not dismiss
the grating of his voice, the way he flew.
And as I left that place I cast my eye
back at its lord and saw his lineage
recede to the Devonian. You lie,
I thought. Each feather is a living bridge.
But Redwing clutched his branch and croaked his tale
as I walked on, eyes forward, down the vale.

The Salamander

Emerging from the flames, this serpent smiles,
Exhibit A of secrets to be kept:
how did, afire, it exercise such wiles?
My bet is, in the seething heat it slept.
That's just a guess. For all we know, it wept
or plotted, came unsprung or filed its nails.
I think it dreamt of laps in which it leapt.
Survival's just a trick when all else fails.
A full report would spare us no details:
core temperature, heart rate, brainwaves—the lot
of data points on logarithmic scales—
and some might think they knew, then, what we've got.
I'll tell them now: a salamander. Chill.
Interrogated, it will never spill.

Jubilate Lupo

For we will consider our dog Magnus.
For he is the servant of We the People and duly and daily
    serving us.
For he pricks us to remember Greatness abounding that he
    alone can retrieve.
For our livelihoods are flown in gusts of wind but we hear
    him summon back the winds.
For our eyelids heavy with the dust of poppy obscure his Messes.
For our ears turned lead by his growls blunt the most
    outrageous Lies.
For he sees far for us with sober eyes and hears keenly for us
    with sharp gold-fringed ears.
For rival packs are wary of his cunning.
For he is less rabid than some of the others.
For he contradicts himself, very well, he contradicts himself.
For he marks his territory without shame.
For he makes shrewd compact with the Wolves to guard the
    Flock.
For we admire brute strength and do not apologize for that.
For he does not apologize.
For he keeps the People's watch in the night against the
    Adversary and sends tweets against him.
For even when tweeting he is no canary.
For the camel cannot rival him in stamina nor the bear in
    tenacity.
For he bounds fetchingly with the poodles in the gated dog
    park.
For Jack London nor John Steinbeck nor Walt Disney could
    invent him.
For the jackals and weasels fear only bared fangs.

For strokes properly applied make him affectionate and genial but poorly applied raise his dander—Poor Magnus! poor Magnus! The fleas have nipped thy flanks.
For we bless the big names on Fox that Magnus feels better.
For fleas have fleas, as he knows, and marshals the tribes into circuses.
For he makes common cause with canines from the tall timber to the steppes.
For he grabs Pussy and does not blush to announce it, and if he did we would not see the blush through the bronze.
For his coat is of a coarseness and a fineness uncommon.
For he can pursue a golf ball.
For he can bite.

Turtles

It's turtles down and down and down and down.
I've seen them. When I looked, they hid their heads,
their shells dipped like the edges of a frown,
their toes drew in. I sensed what each one dreads,
strange raps across the back from up above,
a quiver, as of loose bowels, from below,
and, at the center, skittering toward love
which, yielded to, the whole green spire would go.
And felt what turtles do to stay alive:
quash every harebrained impulse to aspire,
suppress the random impulse to connive,
build harder carapace than next one higher.
Just pause, sometimes, at north edge of a pond
and mind what lies beneath the lolling frond.

Coming Out of Hibernation

for Max Ernst

A bear rubs himself
against a bird
saying, excuse me,
which way to the Louvre?
The bird does not reply!
Instead, a tree fades silently
into the forest,
the bird flies
to it like an iron filing.
Both poles migrate
to one point
on the surface of the world.

The Fascination of Fish

In games of chance, poor fish
speak foreign languages.

The nightwatch is winding
its chain of eyes around the necks
of sleepless cruisers.

A smart brass quintet plays
precisely the same number of notes
as there are scales on five fresh fish.

Not given to friendliness,
schools sigh out their lives, or stray.

The rhythm of the sea
is governed by the Moon,
and the answering crescents
of widely roving fish
are Earth's only true diplomacy.

The Fountain of Beira

> We halted a moment at the ancient Fountain of Beira, but its stones, worn deeply by the chins of thirsty animals that are dead and gone centuries ago, had no interest for us—we longed to see Jerusalem.
> —Mark Twain, *The Innocents Abroad*

Even the skeptic longs to see the tomb
And the way of suffering transcended.
Confessing longing confirms him pilgrim.
Yet, note his interest in the fountain stones
That "had no interest for us," which he splits
Like melons so we see the scooped-out flesh
Of rock and glimpse the lapping herd and flock
And hear the beasts of burden drain their trough.
Trail-weary as these brutes, he leans in close,
Awake to details generally ignored,
Alert for proofs Jerusalem can't give;
Who raked his fellows for the killing pace
They drove their mounts conjures up from stone
Spent ancient calves and foals and bids them live.

The Hall

What illusion doesn't have a future?
Confined to bed, you sat up straight as Thoth
and Seshet, wore his ibis head, her star,
and read, and had me write a future thought
you would elaborate on later. Moon
and reed and stylus were our only need.
One night, Youssou N'Dour supplied a tune
toward dusk that afternoon, you took your leave.
Had you been there, thereafter could I tell?
From ibis and from seven-pointed sun?
From thought that to my sorry keeping fell?
From keepsake on a wall, a talisman?
You kept your counsel close and scribe in thrall
as bearers bore your image down the hall.

II. Blaze Orange

Mirror man mirror me.
—Don Van Vliet, "Mirror Man"

Blaze Orange

Blaze orange, the opposite of camouflage,
creates a bold, conspicuous mirage
of safety, as if iridescence could
not stain with hemoglobin red nor would
it disappear completely under snow
that rushes down with vicious undertow
nor fail to stop or slow a motorist
who'll flat refuse the breathalyzer test.
We bought my blaze orange T-shirt late one year
to spare me being taken for a deer
while walking through the woods. It's comical.
But even so, at least once every fall
I pull it from the bottom of the drawer
and put it on and venture out, secure.

Sleeping Dogs

The dogs stir softly, curled about each other
in a vacant lot rank with drained-out oil.
Their colors, shades of different kinds of clay,
churn lazily as clouds in a lowering sky.
Sometimes I think they're one vast motley cur,
until a boy flips matches at their eyes
or yanks a skinny tail, and they rise
to settle a hundred well-remembered scores.
They'll maul the child that woke them, just for sport,
then scatter out to fall upon the dogs
that crossed them up in other vacant lots,
tonight, amid the clash of railroad cars.
The snarl you'll hear at dark, that muttering,
will be their one congested voice, the din
of sleeping dogs remembering sleeping dogs
and whirling through the streets, the voice of gods.

Salt

A picture of salt: the salient sail,
blood on a plate, cube sugar in a cage.
Salt enters weeping, opens wounds, turns pale,
sells cheap, then winds up on an empty page.
A black cat scales each city's peak of salt
before the grain is scattered on the street.
Whatever happens next is no one's fault,
the table's lust for salt, the tongue's for meat.
Patches of snow smear each salt-sown field,
chalk on a slate where the whitetail flees.
One white plume of his salt lick's yield
flares in his breath as he falls to his knees.
Teeth white as salt, the wolves drag off their prize.
The day they're born, their mother licks their eyes.

Noël

All day the clouds smoke to each other
Over the corrugated roof of the diner,
Gruel gray. I finish chopping wood.
I wash my hands with snow.

Later, walking in the woods,
I give the sign of the cross,
I eat the bad bread,
I drink at the cold stream.

The chips of birch and ash I make fly
Are my friends, the birds I feed
Are my believers, the swirls of snow
About my feet sing kyrie eleison.

How well I know you, seated at the table,
Wondering what keeps an old man strong.
I am a stick in the landscape of the window.
It is my work that keeps you fat and warm.

Canvas

The margin of the morning paper's clawed
To tiny pennants by the paper rake
That dragged it from the press. A headline bawls
Some well-known paintings probably are fakes.
Above the fold? The story of a wreck
Accelerates through fonts of boldface type
Toward some punchy by-line like "Ben Hecht."
The photo's cropped within an inch of someone's life.
What I can't get out of my mind
Are the swallows' beating wings as they feed
On chaff by the riverside. They find
Their hazard exactly equal to their need
And, grounded, keep aloft and filled with lift
Their sails, which bear a new world for a gift.

Salvation

After you've scanned the back issues
with increasing foreboding, the doctor
sees you and says you're good as new.
Back out on the street you go
gleaming with clinical sheen,
delivered again. Time to be strong.
A woman sits on a park bench, reading,
a city forester carts away some limbs:
the familiar unexpected scene.
Your pack of dogs come running,
lithe and black as panthers
in broad daylight, almost navy blue.

The Hunting in Hunting

What were fall weekends in the country for
if not to shut the city in a drawer
with emptied cylinder, hair-trigger locked?

But down a county road a gun club lay
beyond the clay pit for the brickyard kilns,
hedged among wide, pheasant-friendly fields.

At dusk already smothered in deep quilts,
down again with fever or a chill,
I'd hear sharp, singing shots and rolling fire.

They lulled me, these disturbances of peace
so strangely calibrated to make sleep.
Who knew how long an evening's shells would last?

The sportsmen of that era have dispersed,
Chicagoed-and-Northwesterned to a past
now distant as their shotguns' sad reports,

but still a boy lies bundled in that lair,
suspended in a haze of flight or death
as clouds of shot and bullets shock the air.

Dan Campion

The Gathering

Alighting, our crow ducks his beak rootward
for a gander at the landscape beneath
his perch atop the leafless, ailing elm.
He shrugs his wings aloft, backstrokes them once,
again, again, then gathers them like folds
of glossy black umbrella cloth, batlike
but deeper barbed and more pristine of purpose.
He plunges to some prize we cannot see
beyond a hump of lawn, unsavory
no doubt, but to his taste a symphony.
His beak, now fortunately out of view,
pokes roughly in, then pries exploringly.
Here's pemmican, there's marrow bone—a feast.
His wings reclasp in prayer from mishap's priest.

Traje de Luces

What can you do but don the suit of lights
when trumpets blare and crowd sends up a cry?
What can you do but hasten to comply?
The lights will fade, the cloth go musty white.
How not draw on bright garments fitted tight
to perfectly display and dignify
the power in firm shoulder, trunk, and thigh
to wield red cape, then plunge in sword's black night?
The beast waits in its chute to be set loose,
men eager for commotion of its wrath.
You visualize its neck run bloody blue.
So many lights, yet for you just one path
extends before your insubstantial shoes.
I hear you say the suit of lights chose you.

Late

Exactly ninety miles east, a gate
stands open, on it perched a red-tailed hawk
surveying, not the salt-streaked interstate
infested with blurred motorists who gawk
or just speed by, and not the winter slate-
gray sky, not even field of withered stalks,
but landscape of a world immaculate
where wind and prey and canker never balk:
the world of strict necessity is his
to watch with fixity not learned or bred;
no other species of existence is,
or if there was, like moulting it was shed.
We glimpsed him for one instant, like the gate,
which vanished as we sped on, hazy, late.

The Raft of the Géricaults

Their rescue ship is brushed with just one hair
as hint of sail and mast, with hull obscured
by swelling wave and what must be endured,
raft's company of Géricaults laid bare.
The raft's outbellied shroud will take it where
it wants to go: right angle to the lure
of mainmast on horizon. There's no cure.
Some Géricaults gaze shipward, some despair.
The painter thinks of horses running free,
arrays his pride of lions in the frame,
lets racing strokes feed off their energy.
The raft's about to be struck by a sea
of Prussian blue, raiment of lasting fame.
The *Argus* lookouts scan blank foam alee.

Necessity

A flute of bone will sound a lilting tune.
It's easy to imagine *Delta Queen*
calliope set loose on "Clair de lune."
We'll play a dirge on blades of village green
if driven by necessity—a horn
in pawn, a guitar stomped, a clarinet
ripped off from unlocked car, a drumhead torn.
A cat can lose his trumpet on a bet.
A banjo body made of human skull,
that was the most extreme case I have seen.
The twanging was, alas, inaudible,
from instrument displayed in a vitrine.
But have no doubt its sound had sweetest ring
and little children laughed to hear it sing.

The Sleeping Gypsy

Her lion's watching over her, her death
an apparition droll as harmless cloud.
She hovers over sand, hardly a breath
herself, a wraith in parti-colored shroud.
Her teeth are bared in grimace of a smile,
the very teeth of pharaohs at their rest
between the lives they lead, in splendid style,
when Amun-Ra revives their cobra crest.
That grin caught me just now, my eyes waylaid
admiring our houseplants' Rousseau green
and getting lost in forest of their shade,
emerging in her midnight desert scene.
She's seen me stand before her, hunted me,
tame leaves the angels of her sympathy.

Canadas

Each step's a legion, every stroke of oar
A fleet. Each breath of air's charred wood, burnt bread.
The twining river wrings out sun, turns lead
To gold where current laps the western shore.
Some Canadas have settled to explore
This backward section of the watershed.
Whole clans are resting through the noon, each head
Relaxed on pillow of bird's back. They soar,
Perhaps, in dreams, or swim in fantasies,
Or let the river water's hush suffice
To occupy this stopover. A few
Stand sentinel on sandbar or in ice-
Cold shallows, watching as our strivings freeze,
As when, arrested in their flight, theirs do.

The Ant

I heard Galway Kinnell recite "The Bear"
almost from memory but with his book
splayed open on the lectern. His nightmare,
perhaps, was losing track, as luck forsook
poor Robert Frost, Inauguration Day,
and forced him to recite a poem that fit,
but not precisely, the occasion. Flay,
or crawl inside, a beast, you anger it.
Start with the ant, notorious for rage,
endowed with carapace, antennae, mouth
parts terrifying blown up on the page,
and armies at its summons north and south,
for contemplation, as have many gone
before us in the chronicles of brawn.

To Dwell by Water

A heron flies as level as a line
stretched taut between unspooling reel and hook.
No stunts or yaws, no hovering divine
above mice cowering. Just by-the-book
maneuvers, steady as a pilot gray
with many hours aloft on routine routes
whose passengers have never had to pray
while impact warnings played their thousand flutes.
A heron flies as level as a prayer
that knows exactly where it's going to:
one wetland from another, when it's there,
to ask for nothing. That's not why it flew.
A heron's purpose is to live, not ask,
to dwell by water and to ply its task.

The Two Dogs

A neighbor walks two dogs, one on a leash,
the other free to bound across our lawns
as joyful as a dervish on hashish.
I've taken to the thought the dogs are pawns,
one ventured, one held close, protectively.
The leash is short; this dog shows not one sign
it wants to run, but steps phlegmatically
beside its master, never out of line,
while that one lunges wildly down the street.
My other thought is that the free dog's safe,
that is, self-regulated, while the sweet
one clenches rows of razor teeth that chafe.
The truth of it I'd just as soon let go,
as keeping indoors there's no need to know.

Six Robins

Six robins in the cedar branches peck
the berries there and swallow them straight down.
Except a certain robin holds in check
its mottled little globes of blue and brown,
suspending each, a bean in scissor blades,
before consuming it, the yellow ring
around this diner's eye gone shocking shades
of orange. It seems some kind of reckoning.
In any case, no world, once plucked, escapes.
It may be they get judged for size or age
or ripeness. Hard to know, when beak just gapes
a moment, what law serves as inlet's gauge.
Perhaps mere pleasure, lamest kind of test.
They all, it's sure, dye deep a russet breast.

Ice Fishing

The tent out on the lake presumes a man,
a line, a hook, a hole cut in the ice.
With bucket, thermos, sandwich, and a can
of heat, he's built the earthly paradise.
Like Clark Kent, I peer through the nylon walls
and see the fisherman's high snow-pac boots,
wool watch cap, coarse-wove canvas overalls.
All's well. The trout beneath him ply their routes,
and soon his catch will rise into his cloud,
transfigured by blue light and crystal air.
No shorebound looker-on can be endowed
with feeling what it's like just being there.
The drawing up, that is, from cold to cold,
last view the fisher's lenses rimmed with gold.

The Shadows of the Raptors

Those prestidigitating hands must steal
the mouse's calm and hare's tranquility
as suavely as a veteran cardsharp's deal
provokes his marks to raise, then pay to see.
The shadows of the raptors glide like leaves
across a crust of snow, like lives along
the major routes, like fog misting the eaves
on shut-in day someplace you don't belong.
Their point is that they're shadow, can't be helped,
apologetic, almost, as if free
to send regrets. That skill stays undeveloped.
Film noir's their compass, craft, and currency.
We must salute them, keeping elbows high
and bent as sharp as beaks against the sky.

Sharpshin

Sharpshin's a hawk we've never seen. We'd spot
redtails and Cooper's on the interstate,
where, stationed like strict sentinels, they shot
from branch or post or back road's rusty gate
to fish a field mouse from a wave of grass,
or far more often, perched in grim repose,
like officers in Mathew Brady's glass
locked up for good in attitudes he chose.
The sharpshinned hawk, for us, glides higher free
of preconceptions, soars, we'd almost say.
We're grateful, now, for what we'll never see,
appreciative for catch that gets away.
We caught its name, and that's enough. At sight,
who knows, a crooked beak, a twisted flight.

The Entry of the Dogs into Valhalla

It's like the show at Westminster,
Except that all are welcome:
The mutt, the stray, the bitch, the cur,
Whatever woes befell them.
Like gods they enter through the gates
Of Great Hall's off-leash park
And there compare notes on their fates
And run and roll and bark.
All rivalries forgotten here,
All masters kind and wise,
Das Rheingold whistles in their ears
And sparkles in their eyes.
Some spiteful gods, in envy, plot
Low schemes against "the hounds."
But that's their problem. Plain old Spot
Holds Heaven's higher ground.

The Hunt

Tireless and loose, the fox fresh from the hunt
Paced into the shooting club and looked around.
The smoky mantel was faced in stone carried
Across town from the old club, which burned
Down. Enormous leather chairs, like stunned
Beasts full of feathers, stood their ground.

Fox flesh crept beneath its fur like ground
Creeping beneath the paws of hounds when the hunt
Begins. Never had he seen the bears' stunned
Pose, the roebuck horn, the rings around
A screech-owl's eyes so false, so burned
Out. It was a deadly history they carried.

Among the tufted armchairs, butlers carried
Trays and papers through the shooters' ground,
Proferring brandy and news while pipes burned
The obscure, embellished trail of the hunt
Into evening. Sparks lit like blaze marks around
A hartebeest standing as if stunned.

Executed in relief, a stunned,
Startled face of silver carried
The fox's eyes back around,
Bright against the oaken ground
Of the wall, to another fox hunt
Whose echo taunted and burned.

Some primitive fuel in the fox burned
Up with a yowl. Salvers upset and stunned
Servants reeled. Shooters leapt to the hunt
With vengeance, cursing butlers who carried
In too slow the cartridge boxes and ground
Their teeth. The fox glanced around.

Shooting commenced at a moving target. Around
The club the leaping fox drew fire as he burned
Like a stricken tree on high ground
In the woods. Shooters blown with stunned
Abandon blazed at the fox in a haze until, carried
Away, they pumped lead into smoke in their hunt.

The fox was running around outside the stunned
Club as it burned and gasping shooters were carried
Out and laid on the ground. Some died in the hunt.

Who'll Be Chief Scorner?

> *Who'll be chief mourner?*
> *I, said the Dove.*
> —"Who Killed Cock Robin?"

Who'll be chief scorner?
I, said the Critic.
With barbs analytic,
I'll be chief scorner.

Who'll settle the will?
I, said the Lawyer.
Ms. Thrush? I'll destroy her.
Then I'll send in my bill.

Who'll write the obit?
I, quacked the Hack.
I, who know jack,
I'll write the obit.

Who says, I told you so?
I, said the Teacher.
Me and the Preacher,
We told him so.

Who'll gloat without shame?
The Angler affirms:
He stole my worms;
I'll gloat without shame.

Dan Campion

Who'll sully his name?
I, cried the Prude.
His very name's rude,
Yet he ducked all blame.

Who'll build on his grave?
I, said Big Business.
Progress is progress.
We'll build and we'll pave.

Who'll rub out all trace?
I, said Fox Robin.
No sense in sobbin'.
Gone to ground's no disgrace.

Three Elegies

I

The yellowhammer's
red scarf rises through the mist
toward the evergreen.

II

White birch lines the path
that approaches through foothills
unseen fields of snow.

III

A flight of swallows
immediate as rain start
from their cloud, sheer cliff.

Composition

The snow is burning off the roof in wisps
of steam; I know this by our neighbors' roofs.
The first sunlight we've seen for days now crisps
the last unfallen leaves. A lone buck hoofs
it through the backyard's mottled crust of ice,
his black-keys hooves struck delicately, with
a touch as certain as it is precise.
No need of gospel to compose a myth.
The deer's right horn ends in a single point,
the left horn ends in two, a sibyl's tongue.
So which sign should we trust in, which anoint,
aware a hidden bow is tightly strung:
the sun, the snow, the ice, the deer, the bow?
I'll doubt you only if you say you know.

Old Men Fishing

    They swim among reflections   from the spring,
their straw hats   lozenges of scattered light.
      One,   adoze   in a salmon-colored shirt,
starts,   and turns the crank of his reel awhile,
  and nods.   Another nets a bass, unhooks
    the fish,   releases it,   and casts again.
  The oldest ancient   fishes just downstream,
  with a paperclip,   a jug,   and a bit of string.

III. The Mirror Test

*A book is a mirror: if an ape looks into it
an apostle is hardly likely to look out.*

—Georg Christoph Lichtenberg

The Mirror Test

Do facing mirrors pass the mirror test?
The *Mirrored Room*, when viewers step inside,
we have to take our shoes off. Tracks detract.
It holds a mirrored table and a chair.
The point is to exhibit sense of self,
a creature, namely me, so self, a room,
a test, a step-off with held breath, an eye
reflected in a mirror that reflects.
The test is that a mirror come to pass
where nothing like a looking-glass had been,
except a still pool where a mind took shape
and crept inside itself at one remove
and took its first breath, let it filter out,
and misted the self-portrait of its face.

Crows

It is three in the afternoon
And fine-boned crows with feline composure
Cruise through the branches of the elms.
Their wingtips curl in marcelled waves
Like combers ready to break over
Their backs. Gliding through a spray of
Branches they look content as gulls
Dressed for the evening. Margaritas
For me and the señorita,
The sea breeze is sweet,
Shut the door, *Yo te amo*:
They know their lines,
And are too proud to speak.
Down dark avenues of leaves
Their black boleros and mantillas
Sweep to cries that parrot
Spanish grief. The ocean
A thousand miles away
Laps in their figures,
Which glisten in rays of evening sun,
Threads of gold sparkling in their feathers.

Tables

Their latticed rows are turned up in the park
bonfire-high and trim as covered bridges.
The seasoned boards still draw clouds of gnats.
In front of screens of brambled basketweave,
the benches' trestlework writes lines of thick
red exes over browned and crisping leaves.
Late-summer bees harvest powdered sugar,
flies dregs of blood, sparrows poppy seeds.
Waxed paper plates, napkins in gold bands, and
beaded lace that traces winter scenery
spread their cloth below, inside a shadow.
Through the striped pavilion of this shade,
where sparks of hunger blur like shooting stars,
September's creatures drag philosophers.

Interference

Just open a window to the scent of rain
And gnats in amber swarm to life again.
The paleolithically humid and pale
Overcast breeds widows in their veils,
Spider hourglasses telling time
To memory and memory to time.
Concordance of dry myths, the wasted day
Consumes you for awhile, then prowls away.
Full Moon, according to the almanac,
The night's magnetic fields are gray and black,
Its static worse than when you were sixteen,
Its music hectic buzzing at the screen.
The cool sheets heft your blood in their embrace;
A cold hand turns the dial of your face.

"Semantic and Poetic Meaning"

Open on the blond wood table, Kenneth Burke's
Essay orients the contents of the stacks
For a moment, in nineteen thirty-nine.
The cabinets are meeting overseas
To decimate my father's generation.
The sky over London is clear and bright,
As it is in Iowa this morning,
But the diplomats pay no attention.
The window frame's, like wings, aluminum,
Spraying table and book with reflected light.
Impossibly, there's tapping on the glass;
Yellow, with a grass green throat, he hammers,
Eyes what's before him, raps again, flutters,
Whatever he is, whose meaning's perfect.

The Krater

I tell you, the krater is authentic.
I myself witnessed its excavation.
What's more, I believe it holds some magic:
I've listened to it mimic the conch shell,
the sea—even the crinkling of grapevines
that you hear in a vineyard full of sun
on the morning after a soaking rain.
Rest assured the vessel is genuine.
It is cool inside as a seafront cave
and dark as a wine barrel sealed with wax.
Unlike most, those tubs, this narrow-mouthed vase
fit its purpose. The wine and water glowed.
The finish is smooth as an olive skin,
the glaze, miraculously, hardly crazed
at all despite its great antiquity.
The design shows the highest artistry
and taste. No one could fail to appreciate
the symmetry of this arbor, the grace
of the procession toward the sacred grove.
It takes a connoisseur such as yourself,
however, to see the wit of perching
a nightingale there on Daphne's shoulder,
eye wide, beak open, uttering that cry
of Philomel's to quench a drinker's fever.
Should we strike a deal, your hand receives her.

Dalí's Daughter

Her jewelry is eyes awave on stalks at a thousand fathoms
Her purse is the giant squid sifting gulf stream water
Her dress is legions of Portuguese men-of-war billowing in
    silky shallows
Her hair is a forest of kelp trolling bright coral
Her linen is a cloud of ink impenetrable-seeming
Her fingers are torches flaring in underwater caverns
Her feet are spinarettes eluding the nets
Her limbs are the S curves of sea horses
Her clavicles are the ribbons of lion fish
Her breasts are the wings of skates
Her gorge is a conga line of sponges
Her hips are the ribs Jonah trod
Her mons is a dolphin's brow
Her hands are lemon sharks' dorsal fins
Her ears are flukes sounding
Her lungs are the perfumed brains of the ray
Her womb is a school of pilot fish
Her wrists are far-ranging bluefins
Her tongue's the anemone
Her teeth are lantern fishes' brightest beacons
Her elbows are oysters
Her knees are the tortoises that rule the Atlantic
Her pulse is the tide
Her heart is the sea

Sonic Smith

I don't believe in reincarnation,
not this time around.
That blue jay, though, a small sky in a gale,
conjures Sonic's sound.
The MC5 are playing Lincoln Park
August '68
again, this time Ginsberg's cries and jingles
30-plus years late
instead of half a beat beyond the band,
smoky shades unfurled
in Uncle Sam–striped pants and saffron sleeves
against a future world.
The cycle cops astride their blue-and-whites
stood up on their heels
that Sunday afternoon. They gun their throttles
hard, then turn their wheels.

Yanhuitlán

>after a painting by Joseph Patrick

Three Oaxacans unburdening a mule,
flanked by two more souls, a woman and a boy,
occupy the center of a plaza
before the great stone slab of the church,
itself flanked on the right by cloister.

The woman stands near the base of a tree
that leans toward a break in the church façade
resembling the dark entrance to a cave.
Beyond the cloister wall a greener tree
hugs the church tower, pointing toward zenith.

The crenellations of the cloister wall
find echo in cloudbanks looming above.
All is dust-gray and ochre but the green
of the trees and a touch of festal blue
in the clothing of the tiny figures,

los pobres before the temple that stands
upon the ruin of a pagan shrine,
who seem to notice only each other
and their chores, save for the boy, who stares off
at a scorched chunk of rock pale as a block of salt.

Dan Campion

Ode in a Grecian Urn

Truth's tourist stuff, an impulse buy
One day soaked in retsina
We'd chanced to catch a merchant's eye
Out strolling in Messina.

The bargain struck, Cortez and I
Went trotting down the strand,
His leash entangling my thigh,
The urn grasped in my hand.

At our rude inn that very night
Cortez sniffed at its lip
And, finding riches hid from sight,
He roused me with a nip.

"By G—!" I bellowed, like a calf
At sacrificial stone,
"You've cleft my quadriceps in half
And may've nicked the bone."

But stout Cortez, bestride my lap,
Scratched up the mouth of clay
In hope to snag some tasty scrap
Before the break of day.

"Desist," I muttered, and plunged in
My hand, and grasped the thing
Cortez desired: crimped onionskin,
All dewy, like the spring,

And fragrant as a smoking joint
That grateful gods once crammed;
But when I drew it to the point
Of exit, my fist jammed.

"God d—!" I cried at old Cortez,
Now scrabbling at my arm—
Unbated nails, as Hamlet says,
Betraying deeper harm.

I flailed the urn above my head
And, aiming at the hound,
Brought pot and wrist down hard, instead
Upon my raw leg wound.

The urn went smash. Then out there slipped
This leaf (which Cortez licks),
Its Greek key to my Attic script:
"In Naxos, Eat at Nick's!"

Dan Campion

Train of Thought

> *No ideas but in things.*
> —William Carlos Williams

It lacks a designation.
    It leaves a plume of smoke.
It knows no destination,
    Departed as a joke.
Its passengers are sleeping,
    The fireman just died.
The engineer is keeping
    The throttle open wide.
The mail car is burning.
    A crate of hooch explodes.
The driving rods keep churning.
    The flatcars heave their loads.
Conductors prowl the aisles,
    Their lemur eyes aglow
At farmers' daughters' profiles
    In every seventh row.
In boxcars, ruined bankers
    Are chanting songs of Blake's
While cattle cars and tankers
    Hiss mating calls of snakes.
The switchman is a liar.
    The flagman is a drunk.
The brakeman took a flier.
    The watchman's in a trunk.

As renegades and spoilers
    Try taking up the slack
The engine blows its boilers
    And nearly jumps the track.
The children in their cradles,
    The oranges in their crates,
The porters with their ladles,
    Rip past striped, clanging gates.
Ahead, no lantern signals
    The next bridge has a crack.
A red bandana wriggles.
    Its wearer balls the jack.
A station cross the river
    Announces "Train on Time."
The trestle gives a shiver.
    The whistle's pealings climb—
And, pending fraught arrivals,
    The baggage shifts and groans
With tents bound for revivals
    And hoppers filled with stones.

Opposing Thumb

I gaped at *Monkey Business*, pained,
Draped on the couch last night.
The gags seemed trite. The patter strained.
The focus wasn't right.

I couldn't put my finger on
The reason for my swoon
And wondered, Must I linger on,
A humorless baboon—

I feared some misstep sprained my grip.
Thalia's branch is slick;
Might Perelman or Groucho slip?
Absurd. I must be sick.

Then, grunting like a silverback,
I grasped what was awry:
That digit that gives apes their knack?
I'd jammed it in my eye.

Admiration

We can't compete with past. It has the moves,
the confidence of knowing who it is.
Check out those tree-trunk legs. Their swagger proves
we have no chance. It tips all balances—
we're weightless by comparison. It breathes
so slow you hardly notice chest expand,
while our lungs heave and blow, our windpipe seethes,
and even so can't keep up with demand.
We're sparrows to *Tyrannosaurus rex*.
And yet, strange to relate, it worshipped us,
glimpsed flashing wings ahead, would hoist and flex
crabbed forelimbs futureward, idolatrous.
Our flight, past's sacrifice of grasp and reach,
aims always forward, wingbeats that beseech.

Dan Campion

Erik Satie at the Debut of Claude Debussy's *La Mer*

Of "dawn to noon at sea," Satie averred
he liked a quarter past eleven best,
a bon mot equal to his gift for jest
on bass and treble clefs, which, once you've heard,
you can no more forget than captive bird
its native song and can no more divest
yourself of than seabird forsake its nest
above the waves and eddies winds have stirred.
Too many layers of sound that day to count,
the Satie stratum spreads, wide boulevard,
then narrows to allée, then finds a door,
knocks gently and presents its calling card,
climbs up a winding stair to scalloped fount,
and melds sea, city, and green farther shore.

The Cardinal

He ascends the leafless ash branch by branch,
this morning's Thackeray antihero
seeking a mate whose dowry may stanch
his losses and lift him up the bureau.
You'd see him through the Brontës' lenses, though,
and this I respect. Perhaps we can meet
in one of amiable Miss Austen's beaus,
though regimental red portends defeat.
It's scarcely necessary we agree:
Our sky in Iowa dawned London grey.
The cardinal is master of his tree.
Such things just are, no matter what we say.
He trills an air, collects himself, and leaps
beyond our knowing whose wry faith he keeps.

Joint Account

The last check in the pad. Where do you keep
the fresh supply? In bottom drawer, I'll guess.
It's so. But you won't let me have them cheap.
You left this snapshot here for me: confess.
It's you and Louis Sullivan—your smile,
his scrollwork twining up tan clay façade
of jewel box bank, and lion, beaux arts style,
to guard good merchants' trove, winged demigod.
Red brick and window frame of bronze add notes
of value to the scene; your pale blue dress
brings prairie sky. What architect devotes
such care, commands such foresight and largess?
Stone lion hugs stout shield, his claws exposed.
You stand, relaxed as frieze-work vine, composed.

Automatic Writing

A sparrow arrows past the window pane
much quicker than the thought of him can form.
And yet it's "sparrow," "window," "he" as brain
tries catching up, translating to some norm.
Let's close our eyes and write what flies to mind
unvocalized, uncensored, and unseen:
A bird. A pane of glass. They always find
us, even though there's been a change of scene.
You are my bird. You are my pane of glass.
You cross the frame much quicker than I see.
Eluding me, you know I feel you pass,
that arrow flight, that glass synecdoche.
I'll draw words from a trance, a dream, a hat,
but capture you? We know better than that.

The Pomegranate

Its Tiffany insides, its garnet seeds,
appealed to Persephone, as we've heard,
and, as you say, Demeter tears and bleeds
for her. If only those blooms hadn't stirred
in summer breeze and drawn the girl afield,
if only Hades just then turned his head
attending to his own dominion's yield,
instead of ravishing her to his bed.
On single pomegranate seed she ate
below, the underworld stakes its claim
and wins her. Bitter through the city's gate
grind dray and ox cart, dragging in their shame.
Yet winey feast in honor of the dead
comes wreathed by figures pomegranate red.

The Dragonfly

A dragonfly inspects me. Unlike Blake's
ghost of a flea, it doesn't speak. It takes
my measure and dismisses me as of
no relevance. I quite agree, and love
that hovering perspective, parallel
to earth but weightless, girt in emerald shell,
and free to dart and float at will, or what
may serve as will in one so small. I shut
my eyes and take one step: I'm weightless too,
though armored in chain mail of jade. A blue
haze cloaks my shoulders as I pause, appraise
my other, more substantial self, and daze
him with the spectacle of my regard,
at which he takes one step with eyes shut hard.

Dan Campion

Schrödinger's Dog

The cat that's living and not living too
Has baffled millions, and itself. A cat's
Designed for that. A dog knows what to do:
Just bark, and get a biscuit and congrats.

The Cedar Berries

Rain's falling hard. The river yesterday
was lower than I've ever seen before.
Brown, dusty banks prepared to blow away
will suck this downpour deep to hard clay core.
Exposed root I mistook for heron's bill
may be submerged, or break off, float downstream
among the other washed-up things, and will
perhaps fit other eyes' mistaken scheme—
to heron, notion of a trout; to trout,
the shadow of descending hawk; to hawk,
the limb it wove its last-year's nest about—
a root that draws and rubs out glib as chalk.
Rain falls so thick, the air mists heron-blue
the cedars from which fattened waxwings flew.

Dan Campion

Poem for Daylight

Who is wiser than the moon
 seen through snow?
Black swan silhouetted against
 the starless sky.
And who more vain than a mirror
 strung with pearls?
White swan against that cloud.

Incantation

Crow, patch stitched onto
thin air grizzled with ashes:
Be a white cloud. Lie.

Glass Fish

Our school of glass fish poses on a shelf,
reposes there as real fish on the reef
can't do and live for long. Each shows itself
as if to tempt a mouth or lens or thief.
I rearrange them slightly now and then.
The current's sleepy and uncertain, slow,
a curtain hardly stirring. Not again,
they tell me. Let us be. Just let time flow.
They're right. Although sometimes they let me see
the fins and eyes and scales that glistened at
us from aquaria, which whirled a sea
around us, salt, ancestral habitat.
They're smooth but cool in answer to a touch
I mean in thanks they deign to take as such.

Mr. Lucky

> *It's not that you're so lucky. Everybody around here is just unlucky, that's all.*
> —Andamo to Mr. Lucky, the last line in the *Mr. Lucky* series

I've got the album, its condition Fine:
a black cat on the cover, pair of dice
with seven showing, nineteen fifty-nine,
Mancini. Not for sale at any price.
The sleeve's "important notice" still assures
"'New Orthophonic' High Fidelity"
immune to "obsolescence." Music cures
the ills of curators, apparently.
I feel that magic as I stroke the dice
and wink back at the Daliesque black cat.
But spin the record? No, thanks. Bad advice.
A three and four face up. I'll stick with that.
Another roll around the spindle might
tempt luck to turn, the needle scratch all night.

Dreams Are of the Body

Stretched out on the salt flat,
the explorer dreams a forest of glass.
Many join him to live there,
but he has moved to the sea
to learn the slumber of rays and skates,
faces on the aquarium window.
Widows watch for him from their housetops,
but he has marched to the glaciers
to sleep in the ice, dreaming
the long dreams of constellations;
penetrated the rain forest to doze
to the beetles' click and the shrieking trees;
left for the city to lie down on concrete
to the iron tongues of vanished species.
He never sleeps in the same place twice,
in the same position, or with the same wife.
His waking thought becomes, What a tiresome life!
and he lays his body down again and again,
in earth, snow, ash, sand, linen, spice.

IV. The Art of Representation

Many years ago, in the Zoological Gardens, I placed a looking-glass on the floor before two young orangs.... At first they gazed at their own images with the most steady surprise....

—Charles Darwin, *The Expression of the Emotions in Man and Animals*

The Art of Representation

It wasn't so much northern light on flesh
as the window itself, leaning roofs, some
windows facing, that appeared in his frame:
models uninjured by his attentions.

Befriending with ulterior motive
had finally wrenched his palette toward the blue,
and there it stayed through years of slate façades
with cobalt doors and turquoise oculi.

That's always when I catch a painter's eye,
the portrait subject he's been dying for
who just happens to walk by, a second-reel
deliveress his patrons all decry.

He handles me in every sort of pose,
recovering by what his strokes disclose,
and by the denouement he's won a prize.
They're everything you've heard, these artists' lives.

Hokusai in Iowa

    I no longer remember I am here
    there being no mountain
and I at its foot

    reading the sea-level poems about me
    to Grant Wood whose denim bib
rustles like a skiff's sail

    perhaps waves in dirt and tassels
    really are like waves of the sea
so long as we do not think about

    whose prairie if I may be forgiven
    a figure of speech furrowing
at the least disturbance

    craft can always prevail
    provided spokes stick out
from the crucial nubs

    and the eye composes this space
    with composure sun setting
or sun rising

    close to the ground
    nothing fancy, you know
simple beyond comprehension

The Mirror Test

    austere without being witless
   here folk over there scholars
keeping droll actors' suspicions

    drawing themselves out
    into schoolhouse murals
and innkeepers' commissions

    as if after lofty effort
   earth-rubbing lines
fashioned a style

Dan Campion

The Fishers

Under the willow at a bend
A great blue heron studies
The tendencies of the creek
Figuring reflection, refraction,
Acute approach, oblique attack,
A patient angler, lonely priest.

Upstream the belted kingfishers
Preen in sun to seal their feast.

The Exile of Glass

Glass did not ask
and was not answered.
At last it lay down
wearily, and shattered
eyes behind empty windows
beheld a glazed, reflective
world. Dull clouds passing
hurtled at its face.
That did not matter.
Glass curled at its edges,
clenched in a sphere, and
turned stubbornly for shelter.
Glass hid in the mountains
in the company of strangers.
Now we hear of brave deeds
performed by glass, and groan
that it cannot be recovered.

Dan Campion

Muse

We're all lolling in our staterooms, waiting
For the activity director's call.
She'll arrive at ten o'clock, her blue eyes
Shot with yellow flecks of stranded thought,
Her flesh tones copper, rose gold, brass, and bronze.
Her shorts and blouse, white duck and gull-wing bright,
Will flutter trim as sails, whisper-quiet,
Above her deck shoes' single stripes of blue.
There's nothing in this world like a good crew
Discreet with paying guests, no matter who,
And cheerful every morning of the cruise.
We've come to wait on them, to hang around
And do nothing unless they beg us to.
When she arrives, polite, amused, we'll move.

Point and Shoot

Another tourist clutches the railing;
The scene inflicts that touch of vertigo
That makes a thousand-mile drive worthwhile.
Looked down on, time's prolific as the sea.
Across this summer's gorge, the layers fan out
From Ordovician to van der Rohe,
Establishing the backdrop and the floor
For snapshots of ourselves on top of things.

Admonitions

Its object achieved, this is medicine,
Discarding the box of bottles and vials,
Spilling out peeling labels and brittle tape.
It was a long siege, the outcome uncertain.
What a relief to see this rain of pills
And typographical errors absorbed
By the ordinary trash. Fresh water
In a wooden bowl, plain fare, smoke-free air,
Dry feet, warm throat, no taking needless risks
From this moment on, the patient's thinking,
More patient now since being cured.
The family can't believe their stray pulled through,
The scrawny, careless child, the reckless youth.
Still young, they say, still time to mend your ways.

All Your Time

Sometimes you have to go to the supermarket without Walt Whitman.
In the absence of his exclamation marks, the aisles look bare, the families forlorn, the few tomatoes sadly deserted.
The ordinarily garrulous produce helpers and shelf stockers skulk, grudging and inhibited.
They've never heard of cling peaches, they can't be bothered. And just try to find the sunflower seeds.

Deprived of that tan slouch hat and white beard's rays, the most garish display racks dim,
And the longest-fall shambling wig lady appears merely nondescript,
And the new-improved product lines sag their cardboard cut-outs into postures of abject failure,
And the cheez curls go pale as elbow macaroni,
And you wonder why you bothered to tie your shoelaces when sooner or later the string will break anyway.

As the big gray tabloid headlines waveringly visible through the shuffling checkout lines
Suck your attention through their teeth because you still can see the tragic victims they name running in the outfield or vamping at some upstairs club,
Because you're mesmerized like everyone else by the strangeness of all packaging, because there's nowhere else to turn,
Your own teeth chatter to the operatic Musak. Oh it's cold in here between the ice-cream freezer's blast, the air-conditioning, and the generalized indifference, without old Walt's warm, expansive hand to hold.

This is when you find out where all your time goes.
You have spent it—How could you not have noticed?—right
    here at the end of Aisle 8, fretting through your solo in
    the waiting line.
Someday you'll have to get, as the brass-buttoned constable
    used to say, along,
Someday you'll have to learn to remember what's beyond the
    linoleum tiles under the soles of your shoes,
Someday you've got to palm the felt and tilt your own hatbrim
    as you please.

Deflection's Ode

I.

You'd meant to stop for groceries on the way
home, but between the list and the filled sack
you got a notion for an essay
about William Wordsworth Ping-Ponging back
and forth across the English countryside
prodigiously composing in his head
those verses on being here or there before.
Somehow Coleridge and Dickinson tied
in, as if old Whitman held your thread
cat's-cradle style. Of course you miss the store.

II.

The public radio topic is space
exploration by remote control.
An expert says we have to learn to face
our limitations. Some caller claims soul
can't travel by unmanned satellite.
There's a blur of static and then dead air,
perhaps proving everyone was right.
Recalling it was Holmes who didn't care
a groat for other worlds, fair or mafic,
you realize this one's caught in traffic.

III.

With snow now all down, the street's monochrome
as old *Downbeat* shots of Charlie Parker.
The station returns with solo saxophone.
While streetlights come up and the sky goes darker,
some notes you took flutter against the glass
of the streaky windshield and melt away
before you can decode a single stroke.
All those papers you've got to grade for class
kindle in your briefcase like candomblé
candles, knowing you're their puff of smoke.

IV.

A magic dinner cloaked in steam
emerges from the microwave.
Jane Austen's on the tube but doesn't seem
a match for Jay or Dave
much less a foil for "Sonny's Blues"
(that paper on the top sounds bought;
tomorrow run a search for clues).
Digesting what today you taught,
moonlight sluices from your mirror.
No explanation could be clearer.

A Book Dealer's Triptych

1.

His obligations throbbed like aching joints.
That day in Richmond accomplished nothing,
Seen in retrospect, a discourtesy,
Though understandable, for which he'd pay.
What might come next he couldn't clearly see.
That book he'd paged through once, about the leaves,
Rustled through his speeches. He'd have to find
That fellow sometime, have him in to read.

2.

He'd seen his mother in a dream. She'd paced
The floor, anxious for news from Fredericksburg,
Then sat down at the table, where they passed
The newspapers back and forth in silence
All over again. His house in Harleigh
Cemetery would be ready on cue.
He'd grasped his lot of hands, and let them go.
Yet something felt undone he meant to do.

3.

The eulogy, thought Ingersoll, sufficed.
He saw his book of lectures on a shelf
So far in the future it made him gasp.
At breakfast next day nothing dismayed him,
Not the plate or silver, not the linen
Nor even the drudgery of dining.
His derelictions eased, immaculate,
He celebrated *Speeches, Lectures, Leaves*.

The Subject

This fellow Brady surely knows his trade.
A portraitist of corpses will do for me.
Stay still, he says. They need no direction
Who lie out in the fields on which I posed them.

My skull is prominent. Posterity's
Already here in that respect. Mathew
There behind his lens stands fidgeting,
Our wish the same: pain to soon be over.

Dan Sickles holds a different point of view.
Borne, less a leg, up Cemetery Ridge,
He smoked a good cigar the livelong way.
Will his kind carry on when ours is dust?

No doubt, scandal will become the face
Of the republic. We are obstreperous.
It will take long for our image to right.
This bristling visage of mine will stem no folly.

They'll make, perhaps, cartoons of it again—
More like, the civic memento mori.
Mustn't smile. Silent thanks to Providence
My vanity lies dead in Illinois.

Former Tenants

The vacant lot fills with snow.
Last summer saw our old house torn
to laths and plaster, choking haze,
its frame a tangle, wires frayed,
the mildewed roof and chimney spent
a hundred years from being raised.
Winter's landlord now. Tenantless,
warped shingle siding tumbled down
I painted once in lieu of rent,
those stifling, tentlike attic rooms
are blurry prisms wind collects
for auction like unclaimed effects.
That kitchen where the pipes could freeze
while bread was baking finally glows,
redone, in pristine ice, at last.
Here miles away, flakes coarse as ash
unfold their message wrapped in smoke
that burns against the window glass.

Archetype

The white-tile filling station comes to mind,
the vintage one across Pine Avenue
with milk-glass crowns atop the pumps and blue-
tiled border so the walls looked more refined.
A truer archetype you will not find
in Athens, Baghdad, Xi'an, or Sutton Hoo
for serving all their secrets up to view
while still ensuring patrons might stay blind.
The leaded air, paved-over earth, spilled oil,
spent workers—not a sign of these intrudes.
The station's tile façade runs straight and true.
Half a century on, gone gray, it broods,
but stands, a monument to poisoned soil
and water, clean as sketch the draftsman drew.

A Kylix for the Boston Museum

For drinking wine I like a simple glass,
stemmed if possible. A jar will do.
The contents should be of the better class
In either case; put more stock in the cork
Than goblets costing someone lots of work.
For show, however, give me a fired cup
Depicting captain and heroic crew,
A pastoral view, some Thebans giving up
Whatever scene might stir a classic mind;
Glaring apotropaic eyes to scare us;
Or Mr. Lowell aboard his coach to Paris,
His Brahmin silhouette on Pullman pane
The classy black that decks the midnight train,
Fat clusters of blue smoke strung out behind.

Dan Campion

Our Picture with Picasso

He's wearing khakis. So are we. The beach
glows white, the sea bright blue, two sailor stripes
on fifties Kodacolor stock. You reach
a hand his glare translates to archetypes:
a Doric column, ivory horn, splayed fan
and gathered wing. He's giving you that look
the painters of Chauvet cast round and Pan
trained like a searchlight over bough and brook.
Me, I have no agenda, just out for
a walk. Who took the picture I don't know,
some *Time* or *Look* or *Life* photographer,
I guess, who grabbed us like an undertow.
We lived in lens an instant, then lay down,
one frame in family album of renown.

On Aging

The scent of honey locust seedpods, sharp
as coffee, herbal as brewed chicory,
with top note of a lathe turning a harp
at the Lyon Healy works, defines the tree.
You bend the brittle, coffee-colored pod
until it snaps, and you're surrounded by
the compound leaves, the fists of thorns that prod
the bucks and bruins on their way, the sigh
of full-fledged honey locust fronds in June.
Try it sometime, when you're in a wood
in late October in soft rain, or soon
before first snow dry-freezes sere monkshood.
It's practical advice, the only such,
perhaps, that does not interfere too much.

The Fruiterer

I halve an apple, peel a clementine,
rinse berries and pit cherries in season,
slice up a peach or plum or nectarine,
arrange half on a plate, serving for one.
This gives you disproportionate delight,
as if each dawn I'd swum the Hellespont,
when all I do is prep and wrap things tight
so when you wake and rise you will not want
for grapes or kiwi with your toast and tea.
To hear you tell it, people might infer
I groomed the vines and grafted every tree
and ranged the wilds for honeycomb and myrrh.
That master Arcimboldo bid you paint
this medlar masquerading as a saint.

Needles

Ginevra de' Benci gauges with her look,
the one you recognized so instantly
in sisterhood and posted in a nook
from which she coolly now assesses me.
The juniper's black ninja stars of leaf
that ply their needles through the sky, the pond,
the far horizon, constitute the brief
a genius offered modesty as bond.
You met her as a child. She touched your lips
and stroked your hair. The lacing delicate
that seals her dress, the single pin that clips
the collar shut, you saw how primly fit.
You saw bright brow and eyelids trace their arc,
you felt equal surveyor leave her mark.

Dan Campion

Ovid's Metamorphosis

From mealy apple almost medlar-dark
he flowed through stem and branch, became the bole
of heartwood pale but firm and weathered bark,
descended into root, accepted role
of crawling through the dirt for food and drink,
until a pitying Olympian
(it's not recorded which), paused there to think
for once, felt stir where hard-pressed deep roots run,
and, pulling handful up like gathered vines,
teased out poor Ovid, hung him in the sun,
and bid him leaf and fruit, inscribe designs
with winy tendrils, fill up oaken tun.
The man had no choice but comply. The god,
departing, pinched a grape and tamped the sod.

Capture

This picture Barbara took of you so long
ago, that calm and candid look you gave
uncapturable as nightingale's song,
but Barbara did, your lips a trifle grave,
by which I'm sure some gentle laughter hid
until raised up again at your behest,
your hair dark waves the brush reveled amid,
has aged toward cloudiness I can't arrest.
The Kodak black-and-white, subtle but crisp,
shades sepia, your white blouse, ecru, now.
I miss what's lost. And yet here is a wisp
of hair bright chestnut. From beneath your brow
your eyes regard me as they used to do,
as clear as ever, brown their natural hue.

Fedora

Your straw fedora, picked up on a whim,
looked jaunty on or off, its navy blue
silk ribbon hugging crown above the brim,
whose rake befit a skeptic's point of view.
It hadn't cost a lot, was almost free,
in fact, one of those bargains we'd confess
felt satisfying as Algonquin tea
with sandwiches of creams and watercress.
The hat sits on your dresser, catching sun.
I see you put it on again and give
the brim a tug, the crown a tap, the one
that shows, no need for mirrors, where you live.
Lit by the sherbet lights of evening,
that gesture has become part of the thing.

The Picabia Skirt

I've spread out on a chair your mazy skirt,
the crazyquilt your wardrobe didn't need,
I thought, when tempted in the store to blurt
out No if asked. I note how patterns bleed
into each other once again, shark's teeth
against carnelians, purple bull's eyes pressed
to harlequin print. Bronze mosaics seethe,
crop circles flow, an acid trip full-dressed.
You smiled at swirls of compliments you got,
and I smiled too, as if I'd seen at first
the genius of design in every spot
and arc and stripe and diamond-shaped green burst,
had grasped right off cloth's impulse to rejoice
irreverently, and told you, "perfect choice."

Assistant

You let yourself be sawed in half, I think,
to gain the right to liberate the doves,
make sure the rabbit had enough to drink,
conduct the mooncalf on with white kid gloves.
He'd stand there at the center of the stage
until we seemed to make him disappear,
or float up toward the roof, or slip the cage
that nothing could escape from. Year by year
the pigeons grew more feathery, the silk
scarves silker, the velvet tablecloth
more deft to hide the vanished glass of milk
so audiences went silent as a moth.
We played, then, to each other and the fool,
who made invisibility his rule.

Street Views

The Google pictures of our houses smear
across the screen when we explore the streets
we've lived on. Something unexpected greets
the eye each time. Old fences reappear
we thought were taken down. Our cursors steer
us to an alley we forgot, which meets
an avenue we can recall, where fleets
of homebound traffic still grind through first gear.
The smearing disconcerts us like a dose
we weren't expecting served us in a drink
or on a plate by someone with a smile,
and pretty soon we navigate a mile
off course. We're stoned, lost in a place we think
we know. But we were wrong. Not even close.

Still

A moment's stillness is allowed. The pond
gives back a cloudless sky and sun at prime.
With stillness we know how to form a bond
and keep it, so it's here we end our climb.
We're caught in amber. Not one needle stirs,
one aspen leaf, one feather in a web.
The memory of motion dims and blurs
as all desire to change one atom ebbs.
A Steller's jay appears, but makes no sound—
perhaps he's been there but we didn't see.
A silence cannot reach depth more profound.
The jay's transfixed, etched hieroglyphically.
His cry, were he to loose it, would ring shrill.
He's stayed, like we are, just by being still.

Scroll

I tried to speak, but time betrayed my tongue,
or more correctly, agents time had bought,
the damp, the heat, so no word could be wrung
I'd been entrusted with. My voice was caught.
Not caught, exactly, stifled, choked by dust
and mildew, crushed from throat to diaphragm.
Or, to be candid, drowned and burned, as must
befall the misfit flesh you know I am.
A pinch of powder in a cave long sealed,
of silt beneath the keels of striving ships,
of snow that spirals toward a stubble field,
my charge disperses through my scribe's eclipse;
and yet my distant whispers to you yield
the truth of it as from my author's lips.

Acknowledgments

Special thanks to Marc Vincenz for the interest he has shown and for the care he has taken with my manuscript.

Grateful acknowledgment is offered here to the editors of the publishers and journals listed below for first publishing poems included in this volume.

ACM: Another Chicago Magazine: "Sonic Smith," "All Your Time"
After Hours: "Mr. Lucky," "Capture"
Ascent: "Deep Field," "Tables," "Semantic and Poetic Meaning," "The Exile of Glass"
The Atlanta Review: "Point and Shoot"
The Banyan Press: "Hands"
Blue Unicorn: "Suffusion," "The Fountain of Beira," "Canvas," "The Hunting in Hunting," "Late," "Sharpshin," "Muse"
Caliban: "Dreams Are of the Body"
College English: "The Krater"
The Dickinson Review: "Noël"
Ekphrasis: "Correction," "The Raft of the Géricaults," "The Sleeping Gypsy," "Yanhuitlán," "Archetype"
English Journal: "Deflection's Ode"
Eureka Literary Magazine: "Beginning Again"
Flyway: "Interference"
Gaia: "Salt"
Heaven Bone: "Breton Sound," "Dalí's Daughter"
Holy Cow! Press: "Gichigami," "Former Tenants"
Indefinite Space: "Three Elegies," "The Fishers"
Innisfree Poetry Journal: "Fedora," "The Picabia Skirt"
Invisible City: "Coming Out of Hibernation"

Light: "Jubilate Lupo," "The Entry of the Dogs into Valhalla," "Ode in a Grecian Urn," "Train of Thought," "Opposing Thumb," "A Kylix for the Boston Museum"

Measure: "The Cedar Berries"

Medical Literary Messenger: "Exposure," "On Aging"

The Midwest Quarterly: "Picacho Peak," "Turtles," "The Gathering," "Old Men Fishing," "The Cardinal," "Glass Fish," "Still"

Negative Capability: "Crows"

New Collage Magazine: "The Hunt"

North American Review: "Peregrine, Crocus, Aquavit"

Oink!: "Softness Itself"

Old Hickory Review: "The Fascination of Fish"

Parody: "Who'll Be Chief Scorner?"

Poetry: "The Art of Representation," "Hokusai in Iowa," "Admonitions," "A Book Dealer's Triptych"

Quiddity: "The Subject"

Rhino: "The Purple Finch," "Rosehill Park"

Rolling Stone: "Poem for Daylight," "Incantation"

Slant: "The Narwhal"

THINK: "Assistant," "Street Views," "Scroll"

Uncle: "Sleeping Dogs"

About the Author

DAN CAMPION was born in Oak Park, Illinois, in 1949 and raised in Chicago, where he attended the public schools and earned degrees from the University of Chicago (AB) and the Program for Writers at the University of Illinois at Chicago (MA), where he studied with Michael Anania, Paul Carroll, John Edward Hardy, and Daryl Hine. In Chicago he worked as an editor for Encyclopaedia Britannica and the Follett Publishing Company. In 1978 he moved with his partner JoAnn Castagna to Iowa City, Iowa, where they both earned PhDs at the University of Iowa in 1989, and where they were married after it became clear that marriage rights would become available to all. He taught at the university and worked for twenty-nine years as an editor for the educational company ACT. The author of *A Playbill for Sunset* (Ice Cube Press) and *Peter De Vries and Surrealism* (Bucknell University Press) and a coeditor, with Ed Folsom and Jim Perlman, of *Walt Whitman: The Measure of His Song* (Holy Cow! Press), he has contributed poems to *Able Muse, Ars Medica, Blue Unicorn, Ekphrasis, Light, Measure, The Medical Literary Messenger, The Midwest Quarterly, New American Writing, North American Review, Poetry, Poetry &, Rolling Stone, Think,* and many other magazines and anthologies. He lives in Iowa City.

www.ingramcontent.com/pod-product-compliance
Lightning Source LLC
Chambersburg PA
CBHW022148180426
43200CB00028BA/372